How to Draw Scary Monsters and Other Mythical Creatures

Green Android

Illustrated by Fiona Gowen

Published by:
Green Android Ltd
49 Beaumont Court
Upper Clapton Road
London E5 8BG
United Kingdom

ISBN 978-1-912188-05-5
Copyright © Green Android Ltd 2017

All rights reserved. No part of this publication may be reproduced, stored in a retrieval system, or transmitted in any form or by any means, electronic, mechanical, photocopying, recording or otherwise without the prior written permission of the publisher.

Source of Production: Toppan Leefung Printing Co., Ltd., Shenzhen, China
Date of Production: April 2023
Printed and bound in Dongguan, China.
10 9 8 7 6 5 4 3 2

Contents

4 Wicked Vampire

18 Warrior Ogre

6 Bull-headed Minotaur

20 Sea God Neptune

8 Cave Troll

22 Walking Zombie

10 Fearsome Dragon

24 Howling Werewolf

12 Loch Ness Monster

26 Curse of the Mummy

14 Abominable Snowman

28 Frankenstein's Monster

16 Sacred Phoenix

30 Flying Pegasus

Page 32 has an index of everything to draw in this book.

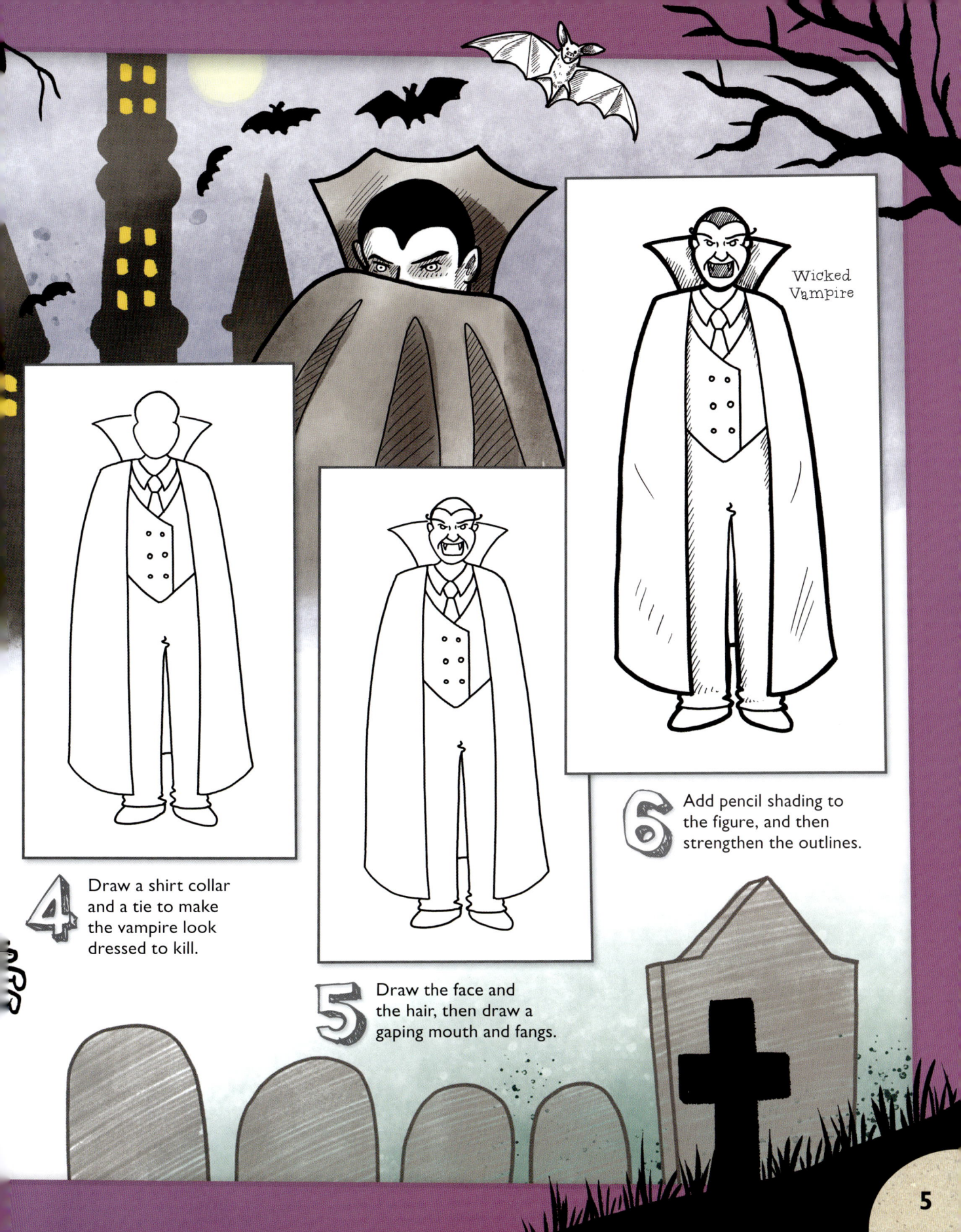

4 Draw a shirt collar and a tie to make the vampire look dressed to kill.

5 Draw the face and the hair, then draw a gaping mouth and fangs.

6 Add pencil shading to the figure, and then strengthen the outlines.

Wicked Vampire

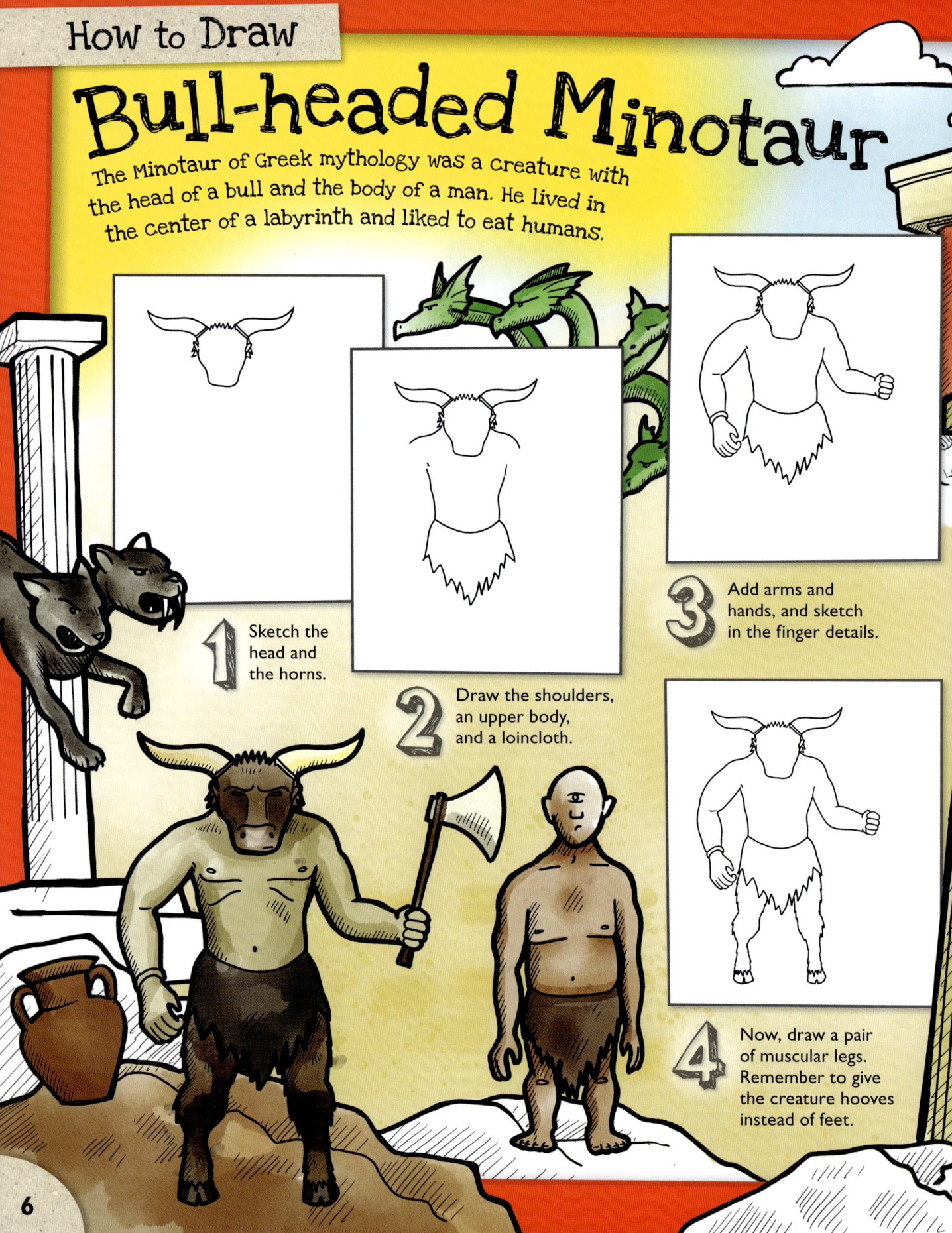

More to Draw
These monsters, which are all collections of multiple animals, have fearsome reputations in myths.

Ichthyocentaur

Centaur

Orthrus

Chimera

Cyclops

Hydra

Ophiotaurus

Satyr

5 Add detail to the face and the body. Then, draw an axe.

Bull-headed Minotaur

6 Add shading, and then strengthen the outlines.

7

 Add facial features and details to the troll's hairy body. Draw the tree stump under his left hand.

 To complete your troll, darken the outlines and add a little shading.

More to Draw
Trolls and goblins come in many shapes and sizes. Have fun drawing these unsightly monsters.

Hobgoblin

Three-headed Troll

Korrigan Troll

Huldufólk

Mountain Troll

Cave Troll

Skogtroll

Leprechaun

Nisse

9

How to Draw
Fearsome Dragon

This legendary creature can breathe fire. It has scales like a reptile, moves like a snake, and flies like a bird. In stories, only the bravest of knights can face a dragon.

1 Draw the head, pointed ear, horn, and teeth. Then, draw the neck, chest, belly, and one wing.

2 Sketch in detail to the fanlike wing. Draw the spiralling tail with its arrowhead tip.

3 Add the pointed tongue, and then draw the hind legs, feet, and taloned claws.

4 Draw the front legs complete with claws, and add in the second wing and the ear.

10

5. Pencil the spiny ridge on the dragon's neck, and add details and markings to the body and the tail.

Fearsome Dragon

6. Use shading and darker lines to complete the picture and to make your dragon unique.

More to Draw
In most cultures, dragons mean bad news but for the Chinese, dragons are lucky!

Wawel Dragon

Fafnir Dragon

Zmaj Dragon

Apalala Dragon

Zilant Dragon

Nága Dragon

Yellow Dragon

Piasa Bird

How to Draw Loch Ness Monster

Some people believe that a sea monster lurks in the depths of Loch Ness, a lake in Scotland. Many have spent years trying to spot the monster they call "Nessie."

1 Draw the head, face, and slightly curved neck.

2 Add the chest, belly, and looped tail. Leave gaps for the flippers.

3 Pencil in the front flippers.

4 Add the downward pointing hind flippers.

12

More to Draw

Sea monster legends span from the freezing Arctic ocean to the warm Mediterranean Sea.

5 Draw some markings on the body, and add a ridge to its back.

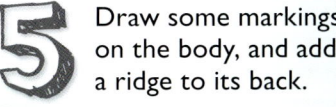

Loch Ness Monster

6 Complete your picture with shading, and strengthen the outlines.

Scylla

Afanc

Qalupalik

Morgawr

Makara

Selkie

Tlanchi

How to Draw
Abominable Snowman

In Nepalese folklore, this creature, also known as a yeti, is apelike and tall. Some people claim to have seen a yeti or spotted its tracks in the snow.

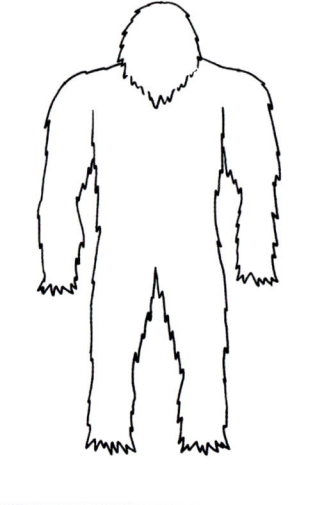

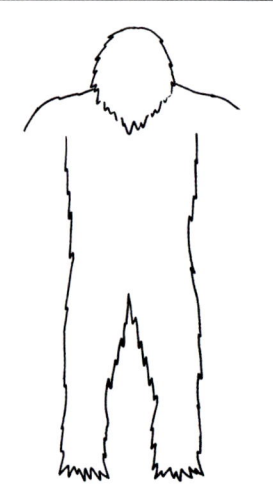

1 Draw the head and the broad shoulders.

2 Use short, straight lines to make the body and the legs look hairy. Leave gaps for the arms.

3 Pencil in the arms, finishing them at the wrists.

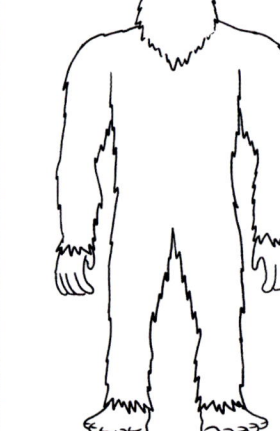

4 Draw large, curved fingers and huge feet. Draw circles to form the toes.

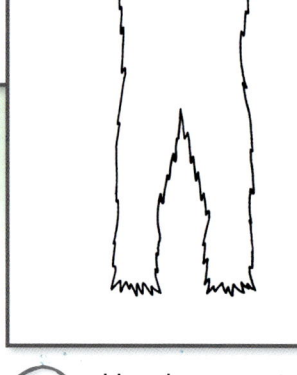

More to Draw

There are legends aplenty of upright-walking beasts that resemble humans and other primates.

5 Use curved lines to give it a stomach. Add fur and a stern face.

6 Add shading to one side of the body and to the limbs. Strengthen the outlines.

Abominable Snowman

Kikomba

Batutut

Hibagon

Big Gray Man

Amomongo

Bigfoot

Yowie

Orang Pendek

15

How to Draw
Sacred Phoenix

In Greek mythology, a phoenix dies in a blaze of flame and is reborn from the ashes. Some texts say that the cycle repeats every 1,400 years!

1 Draw a head, a curved chest, an eye, and a hooked beak.

2 Add a raised wing. Use lots of wavy lines to show that it is layered and feathery.

3 Draw the legs. Finish them to look like ragged pants. Add feet and claws.

4 Sketch the tail. At first it should look feathery, but then it should start to resemble flames.

16

More to Draw

Birds in legends can represent many things, from freedom and love to war and destruction.

5 Add the second wing and the head feathers. Draw tear shapes to create the tail feathers.

6 Finish by lightly shading the body, wings, and tail. Strengthen the outlines.

Sacred Phoenix

Griffin

Firebird

Gandaberunda

Garuda

Liver Bird

Harpy

Gamayun

Fenghuang

17

4. Draw thick legs set wide apart to form an "A" shape. Don't forget the feet.

5. Draw the spiked club and the leather straps of his chest guard. Sketch lines to indicate the ground.

6. Give the ogre bulk by adding shading, and then strengthen the outlines.

Warrior Ogre

How to Draw
Sea God Neptune

This Roman god of freshwater and the sea was also worshipped as a god of horses by the Roman people. The god Poseidon is his Greek counterpart.

1. Draw the head, face, and shoulders. Then add detail.
2. Use simple, light strokes to draw the upper body.
3. Draw one arm by his side and the other bent, with clenched fingers.

How to Draw
Walking Zombie

Haitian folklore is rich with tales of the walking undead —reincarnated corpses—that attack the living. The corpses are made undead by voodoo sorcerers.

1 Draw the head, face, and shoulders using short, jagged lines.

2 Continue using sharp, hard lines for the torso. Add horizontal lines to give shape to the body.

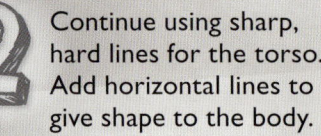

3 Draw the legs with the knees and feet pointing inward.

4 Draw the arms at an awkward angle, and add hands with splayed fingers.

More to Draw

Zombies in all their various guises are not real although many believe differently.

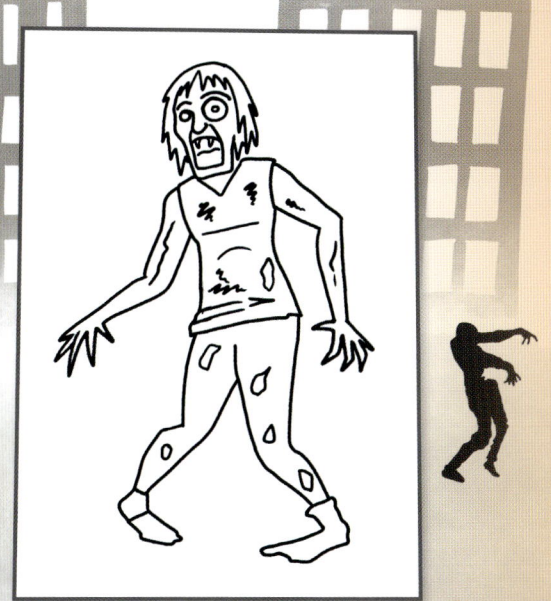

5 Add rips, cuts, and dirt to the body and clothes.

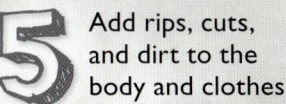

Walking Zombie

6 Shade the inside of the gaping mouth and other areas of the body and limbs. Strengthen the outlines.

Escapee Zombie

Limbless Zombie

Shuffler Zombie

Creeper Zombie

Screamer Zombie

Spitter Zombie

Runner Zombie

Slime Zombie

Crawler Zombie

How to Draw
Howling Werewolf

This mythological beast is actually a human being who can turn into a wolflike creature. Some cultures believe that one sign of being a werewolf is curved fingernails.

1 Draw the head and the face. Note the gaping mouth and sharp teeth.

2 Add a jagged line above the head for shoulders, and add more for the torso.

3 Keep your lines jagged to show rough fur, and add two menacing arms and claws.

24

4. Use oval shapes to give the impression of bent legs. The knee of the forward leg should be level with the claws.

5. Sketch the feet. They are long and broad.

6. Shade the werewolf's body and the inside of his mouth. Strengthen the outlines.

Howling Werewolf

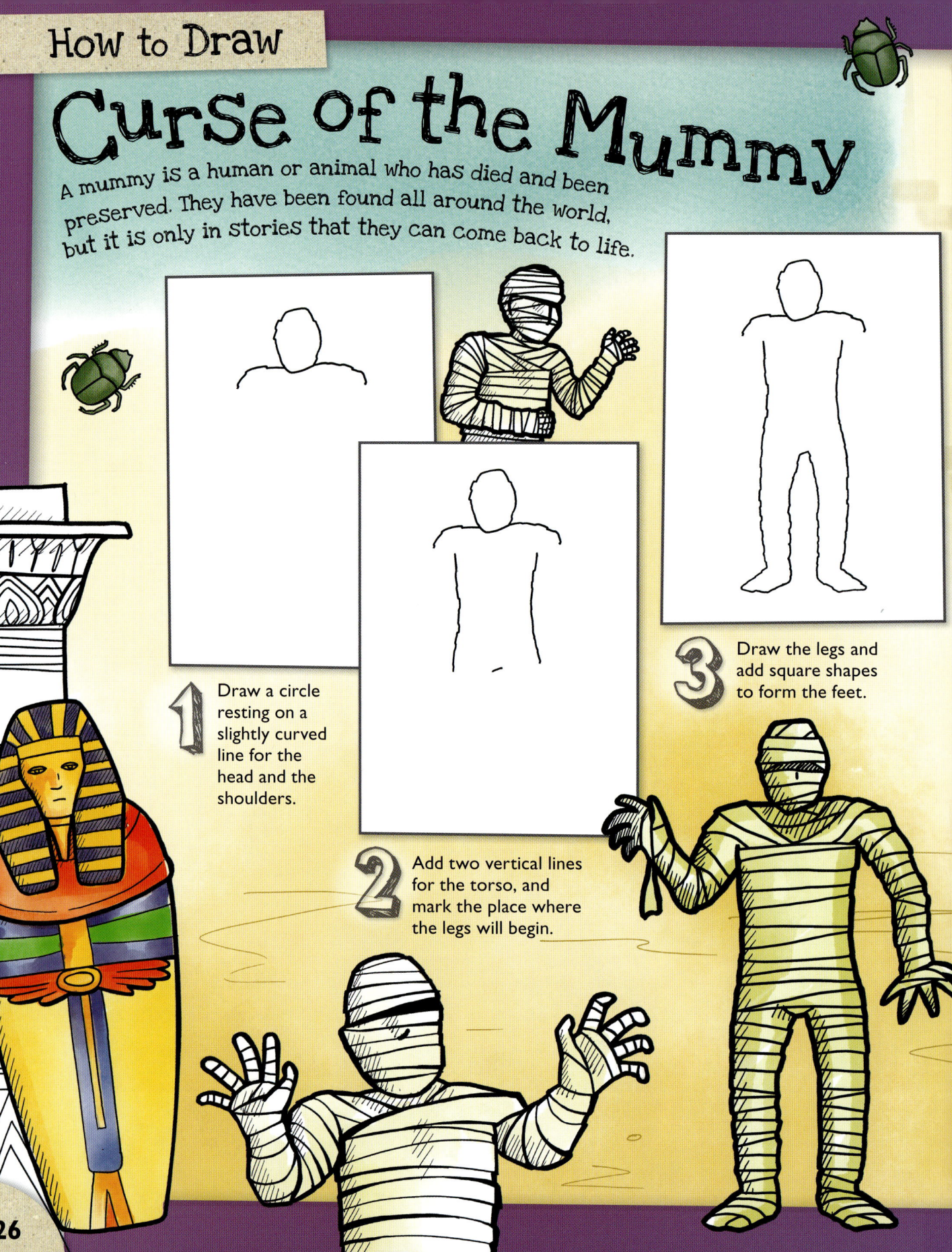

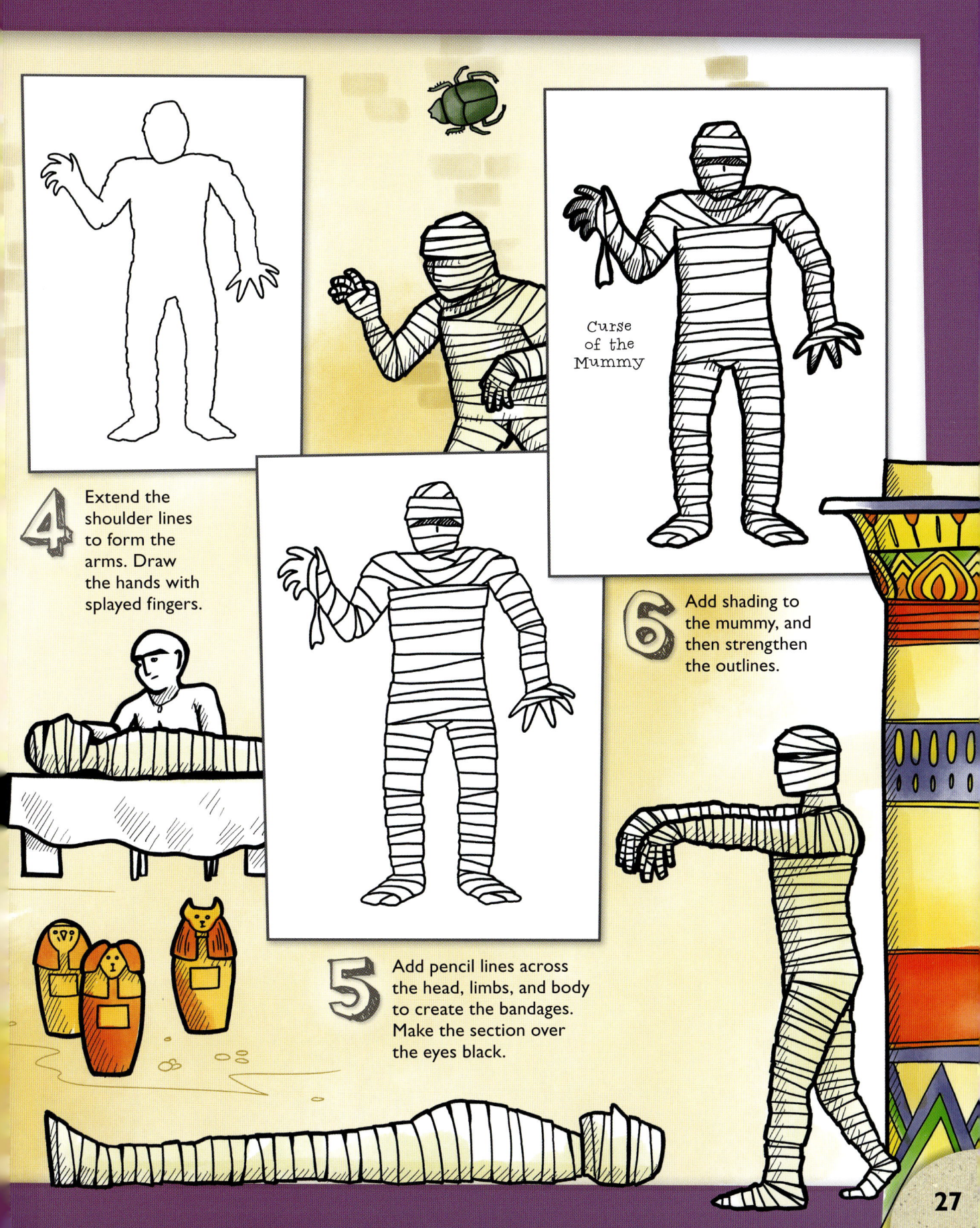

4 Extend the shoulder lines to form the arms. Draw the hands with splayed fingers.

5 Add pencil lines across the head, limbs, and body to create the bandages. Make the section over the eyes black.

6 Add shading to the mummy, and then strengthen the outlines.

Curse of the Mummy

How to Draw
Frankenstein's Monster

This fictional character was created by Mary Shelley in 1818, in her novel *Frankenstein*. He was built in a laboratory and is terrifyingly ugly but very sensitive.

1 Draw the head and the face, then add detail.

2 Use simple, straight lines to draw the jacket.

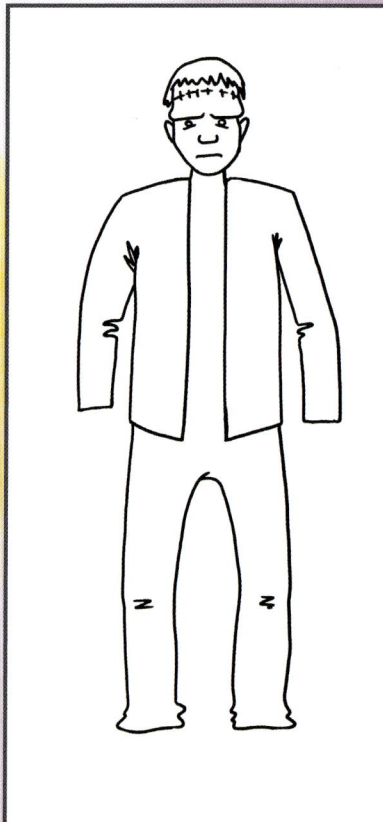

3 Sketch the pants to give him a wide stance.

28

How to Draw
Flying Pegasus

This famous winged horse exists in ancient Greek mythology. He is a horse god and even has a constellation named after him. Pegasus is a symbol of loyalty and bravery.

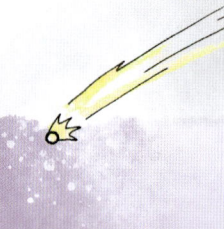

1. Draw the head, neck, and chest. Detail the ears and face.

2. Sketch the curly mane and a raised foreleg and hoof. Draw the belly.

3. Draw the back end, and add a hind leg and a hoof. Note the angles that make up the leg.

Index

This index is in alphabetical order, and it lists all the mythological beasts that are in this book so that you can easily find your favorites.

Abominable Snowman	14-15
Afanc	13
Amomongo	15
Apalala Dragon	11
Batutut	15
Bigfoot	15
Big Gray Man	15
Bull-headed Minotaur	6-7
Cave Troll	8-9
Centaur	7
Chimera	7
Crawler Zombie	23
Creeper Zombie	23
Curse of the Mummy	26-27
Cyclops	7
Escapee Zombie	23
Fafnir Dragon	11
Fearsome Dragon	10-11
Fenghuang	17
Firebird	17
Flying Pegasus	30-31
Frankenstein's Monster	28-29
Gamayun	17
Gandaberunda	17
Garuda	17
Griffin	17
Harpy	17
Hibagon	15
Hobgoblin	9
Howling Werewolf	24-25
Huldufólk	9
Hydra	7
Ichthyocentaur	7
Kikomba	15
Korrigan Troll	9
Leprechaun	9
Limbless Zombie	23
Liver Bird	17
Loch Ness Monster	12-13
Makara	13
Minotaur	6-7
Morgawr	13
Mountain Troll	9
Nāga Dragon	11
Nisse	9
Ophiotaurus	7
Orang Pendek	15
Orthrus	7
Piasa Bird	11
Qalupalik	13
Runner Zombie	23
Sacred Pheonix	16-17
Satyr	7
Screamer Zombie	23
Scylla	13
Sea God Neptune	20-21
Selkie	13
Shuffler Zombie	23
Skogtroll	9
Slime Zombie	23
Spitter Zombie	23
Three-headed Troll	9
Tianchi	13
Walking Zombie	22-23
Warrior Ogre	18-19
Wawel Dragon	11
Wicked Vampire	4
Winged Monsters	17, 30-31
Yellow Dragon	11
Yeti	14-15
Yowie	15
Zilant Dragon	11
Zmaj Dragon	11

32